BRIDE'S

THANK YOU GUIDE

Thank You Writing Made Easy

By Pamela A. Piljac

Bryce-Waterton Publications
6411 Mulberry Ave.
Portage, IN 46368

Note from the author:

I have used a variety of names for the purpose of illustration. Any similarity to actual people, living or dead, is purely coincidental.

BRIDE'S THANK YOU GUIDE: Thank You Writing Made Easy. Copyright 1988 by Pamela A. Piljac. All rights reserved. No part of this book may be reproduced in any form or by any electronic or mechanical means including information storage or retrieval systems, without permission in writing from the publisher. Published by Bryce-Waterton Publications, 6411 Mulberry Ave, Portage, In 46368.

10 9 8

Library of Congress Cataloging in Publication Data

Piljac, Pamela A., 1954-
  Bride's Thank You Guide: Thank You Writing Made Easy

Includes index

  1. Thank-you notes 2. Wedding etiquette
I. Title

BJ2092. P55   1987   395'.4   87-24917

ISBN 0-913339-06-7

Printed in the United States of America

Other books by Pamela A. Piljac

The Bride to Bride Book

*Newlywed: A Survival Guide to the
First Years of Marriage*

*You Can Go Home Again:
The Career Woman's Guide to
Leaving the Work Force*

Table of Contents

Introduction

Why Should You Write Thank You Notes?

For hundreds of years newlyweds have searched for the right way to say "thank you" for their wedding gifts. It has never been easy to find the best words to make the note sound both personal and appreciative.

Now it's your turn. Whether you have 50 notes to write, or 500, the task looms ahead. Although you are happy to have received so many wonderful gifts, you are probably not looking forward to writing thank you notes for them.

Perhaps you are looking for a way out. "Why should I write all those notes?" you say. "Everyone knows I'm grateful. And if they really cared about me, they wouldn't expect me to spend all my time writing these notes."

After all, what would happen to you if you didn't write the notes? You already have the gifts—they can't take them back. People would still speak to you, they wouldn't end a friendship or disown you over a thank you note (unless they're really stuffy). So why bother?

If your thinking has gone that far, it's time to ask yourself—why did <u>they</u> bother? Co-workers, friends, relatives, and neighbors helped to share in one of the biggest celebrations of your life—your wedding. They may have watched you grow up, or shared your excitement as you became engaged and made the wedding plans. When the time came, they went to your wedding, and perhaps to other parties given for you before the big day. To be with you, they may have gone out and bought special clothes, had haircuts and perms, and made special arrangements for babysitters.

And each gift required shopping. They may have spent hours, even days, running from store to store. Or given you a monetary gift that may have stretched their budget to the limit—in order to help you have a good start in your life together.

In addition to offering gifts, many people went out of their way to make this time in your life a special one: Those that hosted showers and parties; Those who ran extra errands for you, or made special arrangements; Your parents and others who not only helped, but contributed financially to the wedding celebration.

They could also have said "Why bother?" They could have justified their lack of effort by saying "What will happen to me if I ignore it all? The world won't end..." I'm sure you see the point. They went through the trouble, made the effort for you. Now it's time for you to do the same.

I'm not saying that you don't want to tell each person how much you appreciate their generosity. I know that you do. But I'm trying to make it clear that the best way to do this is the customary way. You must write a personal note of thanks.

Telling them "thanks for everything" (whether in person or by phone) isn't enough. Putting a little scroll by each plate at the reception is thoughtful, but it isn't enough. Cards with pre-printed verses thanking them aren't enough. Only a personal thank you note can allow you to fully express your gratitude.

This may be a task that you are dreading. You might be wondering how you'll find the time to write them all. You may feel uncomfortable about how to word each note, and concerned that you won't be able to write them 'properly'.

It is very important that you take the time to write to each person that deserves your thanks. What you say in that note is not as important as the fact that you have made the effort to make your note a <u>personal</u> gesture of thanks.

There are only two real 'rules' that you need to worry about in writing your thank you notes. They are:

1. That you write them.
2. That you send them out promptly.

This book won't make the task go away. It <u>will</u> provide you with lots of helpful ideas to make the job easier. It is designed to help you write warm and memorable notes. You'll find answers to the many questions you will have, as well as a special mini-index of the questions and answers for handy reference. There is also a section on selecting stationery, ink, and monograms. Because there are many ways of saying 'thank you', there is also an appendix of gift ideas in the back of the book. Use it for selecting gifts for your attendants, your spouse, and anyone else who made an extra effort for you during this time.

Look over the general outline of what each letter should contain. It will give you the basic structure for a thank you note. Throughout the book I also try to offer guidelines to the proper etiquette for each situation.

When you begin to compose your notes, you will then have two options: 1) You can pick and choose from the list of words and phrases I've provided and form your own note. 2) You can check the mini-index of sample letters and find the one that is the closest match to the gift or situation. Just change the names and use it for your own note.

Finally, the thought of writing 50, 100, or 500 thank you notes can overwhelm anyone. You may feel that you are saying the same things over and over again, and find it frustrating to try and continually change the wording in your notes.

Although you certainly want each note to sound fresh, each guest is only going to read their own note. So don't worry too much about repetition.

Don't think about having 300 notes to write. Just take them one at a time. With each one that you finish, your task will seem easier and easier. Believe me, by the 35th note, you'll be an expert. Good luck!

PART 1

Some Questions Answered

Mini-Index of Questions

Who writes the notes?
Who do I send them to?
Is it enough to thank them orally?
Are reception scrolls with pre-printed thank you verses enough?
When do I send the notes?
Should I wait and mail them at the same time?
What if I don't know the person who gave the gift?
We received a gift with no card, who do we thank?
The gift card wasn't signed, who do we thank?
How do I know that I have thanked everyone?
How can I be sure to thank the right person for each gift?
What if I can't send all my notes within four weeks?
What are the notes written on?
Should the lettering be printed, thermographed or engraved?
What color ink should I use?
What do I put on the front of my informal?
Can I put my maiden name on the informal?
Which return address would I use before the wedding?
What should I do with the left over informal cards?
What about using cards with pre-printed verses?
What name do we use to sign the note?
How do I thank someone for a money gift?
What do I say about duplicate gifts?
What is the right way to thank everyone for group gifts?
If the gift arrived broken, should I tell them?
What happens if the wedding is cancelled?
What should I do if my marriage is annulled?

Chapter One

Your Questions Answered

Who Writes the Notes?

Traditionally, the bride writes the notes and signs her name. However, many couples today share the responsibilities, and some prefer to sign their notes together.

This can be a pleasant way for the two of you to spend an hour or so each evening. It will help you to relive your wedding memories, and give you an opportunity to talk about ways that you can use the gifts you have received.

When you share this experience you will find that the task is quickly completed and you'll have more time to spend doing your favorite things!

Who do I send them to?

Send a note to anyone who gave you a gift; members of the wedding party including ushers, bridesmaids, ringbearers and flower girls; and to anyone who went out of their way to help you. It doesn't matter if the gift or favor was a small or large one, you will still want to send the person a note of gratitude. This includes your parents, your brothers or sisters, and people you see every day.

Is it enough to thank them orally?

No. There is nothing wrong with telling someone that you appreciate what they have done, but it is not enough. A written note of thanks should still be sent.

Picture your friend or relative thumbing through their mail. They find a personal note from you among all the advertisements and bills. It expresses gratitude for something they've done, and will probably make their day! Don't they deserve that special gesture of receiving a note in your own handwriting?

We put a scroll with a verse thanking our guests at each place setting at our reception. Do we still need to send thank you notes?

Yes. Scrolls are sold by many stationers, with verses that thank the guest for being a part of the wedding celebration. They are a nice touch, and they certainly help to make the guests feel welcome, but they do not replace a personal thank you note for each gift received.

When do I send them?

As soon as possible. If the gift arrives up to one week before the wedding, you should send your note within three weeks of its arrival. If you receive the gift after that, four weeks after the wedding (or honeymoon if it immediately follows the wedding) is considered the maximum acceptable delay in sending out your notes.

A note that arrives months after the occasion lacks enthusiasm. It is also inconsiderate, because it leaves the giver wondering if you received the gift or not.

Remember that these people may have spent hours shopping for your gift. They may have planned their budget carefully to give you a special monetary present. They are not expecting too much when they hope to hear that you enjoyed receiving what they gave you.

It will also be easier to write the notes if you do it while everything is still fresh in your mind.

Here are some time-saving ideas:

1. Write your notes as the gifts arrive.
2. Pre-address your thank you note envelopes when you address your wedding invitations.
3. Have a system of recording gifts to keep track of names and every item received.
4. Write a description of the gift as you receive it. For example: 'A hand-painted oriental statue with intricate floral designs'. These will be great to refer to when you write your notes.

It will take me several weeks to get all of the notes done. Should I mail them as I write them, or hold them and mail them at the same time?

If the gift is received before the wedding, mail the note as you receive the gifts. After the wedding, you might want to mail them together, or in batches. If you don't mail them together, try to sort them so that neighbors, friends, and close relatives all have their notes mailed the same day. It may seem like too much trouble, but if you don't your phone may start ringing with questions like "Mary received her thank you note today and I didn't. Did you receive my gift?"

What if I don't know the person who gave the gift?

You would still send a thank you note. If the gift was received before the wedding, there's a good chance that you will meet the person at the wedding, or at a pre-wedding party. Mention that you are looking forward to seeing them at that occasion.

If the gift was received after the wedding, check with your husband and the parents on both sides. It's possible that you were introduced, but are unable to remember this person. It's easy for that to happen in the excitement of the wedding day, especially if you had a large reception.

If everyone is unclear as to who the person is, just thank them for the gift. Maybe they went to the wrong wedding!

We received a gift that had no card with it. Who do we thank?

Cards and gifts can become separated, and it isn't always easy to find the right person to thank. First, check with anyone who was with you when you opened the gift. They might remember a card being with it and who it was from. If that doesn't work, ask both sets of parents and other close relatives. The giver might have told one of them about their gift. As a last resort, go through your invitation list. You can cross off the names of each person known to have given you a present. Hopefully, there will only be one name left when you're done. Thank them for the gift.

We received a monetary gift but the card wasn't signed. Who do we thank?

This is the most difficult gift to trace. The only real solution is to go through your invitation list, in the same manner as above. You can cross off the names of each person known to have given you a present. Hopefully, there will only be one name left when you're done. Thank them for the gift.

How do I know that I have thanked everyone that I should have?

Sit down and think about the past six months. Who went out of their way to help you? Who gave you a shower or party? Make a list of all the names, and don't forget your parents and your wedding party.

When thanking people for gifts, it is possible for someone to be forgotten. Perhaps their index card was lost, perhaps the gift arrived without a card or unsigned. You might have accidently crossed their name off your list. After a month or so has passed, the 'forgotten' person might mention to a parent, aunt, or grandparent "It's not that I need a thank you, I just want to be sure they received the gift." When that happens, you'll probably hear about it and can rectify the matter at once.

Chapter Two

Make It Easy With A System

How can I be sure to thank the right person for each gift?

You need a system. The two most popular among brides are the file card system, and the notebook system. You can also buy fancier bound books to record the same information from any stationer. I will briefly describe each option here.

File card system: I prefer these cards over the notebook system. For one thing, you can easily alphabetize the cards for quick reference later.

Then if you need to know "Did I send Mrs. Brown her thank you note?" or "What gift did Mr. & Mrs. Roberts send us?" You can quickly find your answer by flipping through the cards.

Since you'll be receiving more than one present from many of these people (engagement, wedding shower, personal shower, wedding) I believe it is easier to record all of your gifts in the same place.

For example, many notebooks separate wedding and shower gifts. This requires you to do extra recording, sorting and addressing. With the note cards you can record everything together.

You can purchase blank 3 × 5 index cards and draw in your own lines and headings. Or some gift shops sell pre-printed cards for this purpose. Here is an example you may use:

Name		
Address		
Occasion	☐ Thank You sent	Date
Brief description of gift		
Occasion	☐ Thank You sent	Date
Brief description of gift		

You will also want to thank those people who did special favors for you, as well as those who gave parties, dinners, or showers in your honor. Be sure to note these special gestures on the back of their gift record card.

Notebook System: You can record the same information in a bound or looseleaf notebook. Just be sure to include:

1. The name and address.
2. Occasion and date received.
3. Brief description of gift.
4. If thank you note sent.
5. When thank you note sent.

Whichever system you use, make a note near the name, or on the back of the card each time you invite someone over, or mention similar plans in your thank you note. You need to have some kind of record of all your promises!

Help! I had six hundred people at my wedding. There is no way I can send all my thank you notes in four weeks. What should I do?

When you have a very large wedding, or if you plan a long honeymoon, it may not be possible to acknowledge all of your gifts within four weeks. In that case, you can send a pre-printed card (address them before the wedding) acknowledging receipt of the gift as it arrives. This lets the giver know that you have safely received the gift. However, these cards would not be a substitute for your thank you notes. You should still send a personal note as soon as you are able to get them written. Here are some ideas for the wording on the pre-printed cards:

*Karen Smith and Michael Jones
wish to acknowledge the receipt
of your thoughtful wedding gift.
A personal note of thanks will be
sent at a later date.*

OR

*Mr. & Mrs. Michael W. Jones
wish to acknowledge the receipt
of your thoughtful wedding gift.
A personal note of thanks will be
sent at a later date.*

Chapter Three

Stationery/Informals

What are the notes written on?

Like all stationery for your wedding day, the style of Thank You that you choose should suit the formality of your wedding. There are several kinds of stationery you can choose from:

1. Blank cards with the words *"Thank You"* pre-printed on the front are sold for this purpose everywhere. According to the 'rules' of etiquette, these cards would only be used for small, informal weddings. However, many couples prefer to use them anyway.

2. Cards with your wedding photograph on the front can be obtained through most stationers. The inside would include a blank area where you would write your note. These cards double as a delightful keepsake souvenir of your wedding! Since it takes time for the photograph to be developed and reproduced, select a card that has a slot where you can slip the picture in at a later date. That way you can write the notes ahead of time, and just add the pictures when they are ready.

3. If you have a formal wedding, proper etiquette requires the use of the traditional thank you note. These are written on 4×5 cards called "informals". They would match your wedding stationery, and you can order them when you order your invitations. These cards will have your name, your spouse's name, or a monogram on the front.

Selecting your personal stationery

When choosing your informal cards, you would use the same type of paper that your wedding invitations are printed on.

You can select your personal stationery for use after the wedding at the same time. There are many types and styles of paper to choose from.

Whether it is rich, thick vellum or a thin paper with a brightly colored design, the paper should reflect your personality and your pocketbook.

And once you have selected the paper, here are several other points to consider while making your decision.

Should the lettering be printed, thermographed or engraved?

Offset printing is the least expensive method. A rubber cylinder transfers the inked letters to your paper. This type of printing would not be used on informals. It can be used on personal stationery, but it does not have the elegant look that the other methods have.

Thermography (also called 'raised lettering') looks similar to engraved lettering. The letters are made by combining ink and powder, and they have the raised effect of engraved lettering. It is a less expensive process, and can be done more quickly than engraving. When properly done, only those people who are familiar with engraved stationery can tell the difference between thermo-engraved and engraved.

Engraving is raised lettering that feels very elegant when you touch it. It costs quite a bit more than the thermo-engraving process. If you are having a very formal wedding, it is still considered important that the wedding stationery be engraved. This method may not be as expensive as you think. If you will be re-ordering informals or other personal stationery with the same wording after the wedding, you can re-use the die. Since there is a large initial charge for making the die, the real cost of engraving can be factored over the future uses you may have of it.

Selecting your ink color

You can have your informals or your stationery imprinted with any color ink imaginable. However, black is the traditional, formal color to use. Here are just a few others you might select: blue, turquoise, brown, gold, purple, lavender, maroon, gray, silver, rose and peach. Bear in mind that most stationers will add an additional charge for any ink color other than black or blue.

What do I put on the front of my informal?

Traditionally, it is your married name, the way that you expect to be addressed, such as:

Jillian Hubbard Martin

Ten years ago, it was considered wrong for an informal to bear more than one name, and only one name was signed to the note. However, more and more couples today have broken with this tradition and sign their notes together. You might list your names as:

Mr. and Mrs. Daniel Robert Martin

OR

Jillian and Daniel Martin

If you plan to use informals, you still shouldn't use any that have your new husband's name on them until after the wedding. If you hope to have some thank you notes written and sent before the wedding, you would have your maiden name imprinted on the card, such as:

Sarah Elizabeth Smith

If your future husband helps you to write the notes before your wedding day, his cards should show his name only, such as:

Jeffrey Allen Jones

Many people prefer their informal cards to bear a monogram. Some couples use both names and an initial in the center, such as

---

Katherine

R

David

Generally, just two or three initials are used in a monogram, especially if only one person will sign the card or letter.

There are many different kinds of personal monograms. If you aren't married yet, you would use the initials of your first name, middle name and maiden name. As a married woman, you would use the initials of your first name, maiden name and married surname. As a married man, you would use the initials of your first, middle and last name. Some people pay to have their monogram designed especially for them, or copy patterns they have seen on linens or silverware.

What if I plan to keep my maiden name after the wedding?

Put both names on the front of the informal card, one above the other. For example:

Karen Lynn Walters
Michael Wayne Davis

Which return address should I use before the wedding?

The writer would use their own return address. If you know what your address will be after the wedding, it's a nice idea to include it as part of the note.

What should I do with any informal cards that are left over?

Keep them. Informals with your married name(s) on them can also be used after the wedding to:

- Send brief notes
- Accept or decline invitations
- Write thank you's for other occasions
- As informal invitations
- As gift enclosure cards

What about using cards with pre-printed verses?

There are cards being sold that have words of thanks already printed inside. You can even have your name pre-printed on the bottom. The only thing you have to do is to address the envelope. These may sound like great time-savers, but please don't use them. The only time they are acceptable is if you send a personal note *after* sending the card.

One of the nicest things about receiving a thank you note is the personal appreciation that it shows. A pre-printed verse means nothing to the person who receives it. At best, it acknowledges that the gift was received. But it looks as if you are only going through the motions of what is expected of you. It certainly doesn't reflect any true gratitude on your part.

The few minutes that you take to write a friendly note will mean a great deal more to the person who gave you a gift, or did special favors for you.

PART 2

Writing
The
Note

Chapter Four

General Outline

Writing the Note

Choose an ink color that is easy to read such as blue or black. Try to write as legibly as possible. Make each note sound like you. Don't use words that you feel uncomfortable with, or that you wouldn't usually say. You don't have to use formal, stilted language. Just be yourself.

A good trick is to try and picture the person you are writing to in your mind as you are composing the note. It will make it easier to speak directly to them in the same way that you usually do.

The note doesn't have to be long. A few lines that are brief but sincere are all that is necessary. Reading it should make the receiver feel as if you were writing to them personally. This isn't always easy, especially when you are writing fifty of them at a time. But no matter how tired you are, try to make each note sound like it is the only one you are writing.

General Outline

The basic structure of each note would be:

☐ Address the person you are thanking.

☐ Note who is giving thanks.

☐ Mention something nice about the gift.

☐ Tell a way that you might use the gift.

☐ Make a final pleasant comment.

☐ Thank them again.

☐ Sign off.

Now let's cover these in more detail:

Address the person you are thanking: Traditionally, the note is addressed to the wife and the husband is mentioned in the note. Many couples now prefer to address the note to both husband and wife.

Other than that, the best general rule to follow is to address each note as you would normally greet that person: whether it's Mr., Aunt, or by their first name. If you are writing to your new spouse's relatives, address the person as he or she would. Here are some ideas for addressing the note:

Dear Mrs. Donaldson
Dear Mr. and Mrs. Donaldson
Dear Dan and Sarah,
Dear Aunt Paula
Dear Mickie,

When writing thank you notes to a large group, just address it to "Dear Friends" or "Dear Co-Workers" (or whatever their relationship may be to you or your spouse).

Note who is giving thanks: This is identifying who the note is from. For example: "I", "Jeffrey and I", "Karen and I" or "We".

Thank them: When you write a lot of notes, you start to run out of ways to say thank you. Or you may want to include your thanks in several different ways in one note. Here are some ideas:

- Daniel and I would like to thank you...
- Jill and I are very grateful...
- We were so delighted when we opened your gift of...
- Dan and I appreciate...
- Karen and I were excited to receive...
- Jeff and I were so pleased when we...
- Daniel and I can't thank you enough...

Mention something nice about the gift: It isn't easy coming up with enough original adjectives and descriptions for your wedding gifts. Remember to mention the gift specifically. Don't just thank them for their 'gift'. Thank them for the crystal vase or the silver tea set. If you are not sure what the gift is, describe it. For example:

Karen and I can't thank you enough for the beautifully carved wooden statue.

Here are some other descriptive words to pick and choose from when writing your notes:

- ☐ Lovely
- ☐ Attractive
- ☐ Generous
- ☐ Perfect
- ☐ Handsome
- ☐ Useful
- ☐ Thoughtful
- ☐ Fascinating
- ☐ Magnificent
- ☐ Glamorous
- ☐ Eye-Appealing
- ☐ Exquisite
- ☐ Appropriate
- ☐ Sparkling

- ☐ Special
- ☐ Elegant
- ☐ Beautiful
- ☐ Pretty
- ☐ Decorative
- ☐ Delightful
- ☐ Impressive
- ☐ Exotic
- ☐ Charming
- ☐ Superb
- ☐ Stunning
- ☐ Much-needed
- ☐ Valuable
- ☐ Embossed

- ☐ Future heirloom
- ☐ Sculptured pattern
- ☐ Beautifully carved
- ☐ Life-like details
- ☐ Intricately detailed
- ☐ Delicate design
- ☐ Antique finish
- ☐ Fine embroidery

- ☐ Ornate design
- ☐ Floral detail
- ☐ Hand painted
- ☐ Multi-purpose
- ☐ Swirled glass
- ☐ Classic style
- ☐ Polished brass
- ☐ Unique design

Mention a use for the gift: No one wants to think that their gift will be stuck away in a closet for the next twenty years. Think of a way that you will be using the gift and try to work it into the note. Here are some ideas:

- This. . . is such a welcome addition to our collection of. . .

- The. . . is perfect for entertaining guests.

- We'll enjoy using. . . on special occasions.

- This. . . will save us so much time because. . .

- . . . is ideal for our new home because. . .

- The. . . really brightens up our. . . room.

- This. . . is so versatile, I can't begin to list all the ways we can use it!

- I can't believe how well the. . . suits our decor.

- The. . . will come in handy when. . .

- . . . is a distinctive accessory for our. . .

- It is an ideal accent piece for. . .

- This. . . will be fun to use.

- I can't wait to try. . . the next time we. . .

- The. . . will help us to organize. . .

- We will always treasure this. . .

- Everyone who comes into our apartment will admire the. . .

Make a final pleasant comment: You want to reinforce your thanks with an extra line. Here are some more ideas:

- The. . .is just what we need for. . .
- We will give the. . .a place of honor in our home.
- Just knowing how carefully you selected the. . .
- This. . .is exactly what we wanted. . .
- It means so much to us that you went out of your way to find this. . .
- We are so proud to own this. . .
- We hope that you will visit soon to see how wonderful the. . .looks.

Thank them again:

- Thanks to you. . .
- Thanks again for. . .
- Again, many thanks. . .
- We can't thank you enough. . .
- I am so gratified that. . .

Sign off: The words you choose will depend on your relationship with the addressee, and the way you began the note. A note that begins "Dear Mr. and Mrs. Jones" shouldn't be signed "with love and kisses". Here are some ideas for concluding:

- Love
- Affectionately
- Sincerely
- Cordially
- Truly yours
- Fondly
- With affection
- Lots of love
- Love always
- Your friends
- Best Regards

Chapter Five

More Questions Answered

What name do we sign the note with?

Traditionally the bride signs the note. Before the wedding she signs her maiden name, after the wedding her married name. However, most couples today sign their notes jointly.

You should sign by first name(s) only if you are positive that they will know who you are. A great deal depends on your relationship with the addressee, and how you wish to be addressed after the wedding. Here are some options:

Jill and Jeff

Jillian Marie Swanson

Jeffrey Allen Hubbard

Mrs. Jillian Hubbard

Mrs. Jeffrey Hubbard

Jillian Swanson Hubbard

Mr. & Mrs. Jeffrey Hubbard

Jillian Swanson and Jeffrey Hubbard

How do I say "thank you" for a money gift?

Refer to it as 'generous' or 'thoughtful'. Include an explanation of what the money will be used for. Don't mention the actual dollar amount of the money that you received.

What do I do when I receive duplicate gifts?

No matter how carefully you register your choices, it's almost inevitable that you will receive more than one of the same item. Although there is nothing wrong with exchanging duplicate gifts, it is considered impolite to tell the giver that you have done so. You might receive four toasters, six ice buckets or two identical crystal vases. Even if your guests are aware of the duplication, each person wants to believe that you would rather keep theirs and exchange the other gift(s). So write your note thanking the person for the actual gift they gave you, not what you traded it in for.

What about joint gifts?

Some friends or family members like to pool their funds to buy a larger gift. The way you address the note will depend on the number of people who went together on the gift. The general rule is that for less than six, each individual should receive their own note. Don't make them identical—a word change here or there will make it more personal. If more than six people buy one gift (such as co-workers) you can send a group note addressed to all of them. A group note should only be sent to people who are generally found in one place—such as an office. There, the note could be circulated or displayed for all to see.

We received a broken gift. Should we tell the giver?

It's heartbreaking when something like that happens. However, it's best <u>not</u> to tell the giver that their present was ruined. It will only disappoint them, and make them feel awkward. If it was shipped directly from the store, you might contact the store manager and explain the situation. Some stores will replace the merchandise. If that's not possible, just thank the sender for the gift without mentioning it's status.

What happens if the wedding doesn't take place, or if the marriage is annulled very quickly? Do I still write thank you notes? Must I return the wedding gifts?

If for some reason the engagement is broken, the wedding does not take place, or an annulment is granted almost immediately after the wedding, all gifts should be returned to those who sent them. The only exceptions would be trivial, inexpensive shower gifts. If the marriage was annulled you would only return unused gifts.

You may feel uncomfortable writing a note of explanation, but a brief tactful note is all that is necessary.

If the gifts are returned, the bride-to-be would write to her friends and family, the groom-to-be would be responsible for writing to his. If a gift was given by someone who is friends to both, the bride would write the note and return the gift.

You will find sample letters for this situation in the back section of the book.

PART 3

Sample
Letters

Index of Sample Letters

Chapter 7 General Letters

Chapter Six

Specific Letters

#1   Monetary Gift

Dear Aunt Karen,

Thank you for the generous check! We used it for something very special.

We chose a beautiful rocking chair that fits perfectly into the corner of our living room. It is truly the nicest piece of furniture we own! We plan to slowly add other pieces as time goes on—and build our room around the chair.

We can't thank you enough for your kind and thoughtful present. Please come over soon so that you can try it out!

Love,

Peggy and Tim

#2 Monetary Gift

Dear Marcie and Scott,

Thank you for your generous wedding check. Ken and I have been saving for a new television, and your gift will help us to buy the set we've been eyeing for some time. It has a good sized screen, so we'll be expecting you over to watch the Cubs play!

Thanks again. We're both looking forward to seeing you at the wedding!

Cordially,

Karen and Ken

#3 Monetary Gift

Dear Grandma and Grandpa,

Thank you, thank you, thank you for the generous wedding check! It was such a wonderful surprise. Jeff and I have added it to our special savings account for a new car. Thanks to you, we'll be shopping for one next week. I'm so glad that we can finally get rid of my old clunker.

We are so grateful to you, and we'll be driving over to give you a ride in our brand new car very soon!

Love

Karen and Mickie

#4 Monetary Gift

Dear Mr. and Mrs. Reynolds,

Laurie and I appreciate your nice check. We had been looking all over for a coffee table that will fit into our tiny living room. We finally found one last week. Your gift will help us to bring it home.
We were glad to see you at the wedding, and we only wish we could have spent more time with you. But as you know, it was a pretty hectic day!
Thank you again for being so generous!

Sincerely,

John and Laurie Peterson

#5 Monetary Gift

Dear Aunt Florence,

Steve and I appreciate your generous gift, and plan to us it towards a set of dinnerware. We have a set all picked out, they are just what I've always wanted. I can't wait to show them to you!
Thank you so much for your good wishes too! We are so glad you were able to come to the wedding, and hope to have you over for dinner soon so you can 'inspect' our purchase.

Love,

Sarah and Matt

#6   For party or dinner given in your honor

Dear Dan and Becky,

Mickie and I want to thank you for the wonderful dinner last night. The food was fantastic—did you really cook it all yourself? We definitely savored the results!

This is such a hectic time for us, and it was nice to relax with the best friends anyone could have.

Thank you for caring enough to do this, we know how busy you are. You're the greatest!

Love,

Sarah and Mickie

#7   For party or dinner given in your honor

Dear Mr. & Mrs. Thompson,

Karen and I were so surprised last night! We can't thank you enough for the wonderful evening. How did you manage to keep it all a secret?

We were delighted that John agreed to sing—thanks for talking him into it. It's so great to work for a company that cares so much for their employees. We can't wait to see you at the wedding.

Thanks again—it was a party that we'll never forget!

Best Regards,

Richard M. Reynolds

#8   For party or dinner given in your honor

Dear Sandi,

Thank you so much for arranging a luncheon party for me. It was so much fun—and a nice break from all the headaches of planning a wedding. You certainly know how to treat a friend!

I just loved those little pastries you served! Please give me the recipe. I could eat those every day, and I know that Rob would love them too. I am really grateful for the wonderful time. Thanks again and again!

Love,

Sarah

#9   For Rehearsal Dinner

Dear Mom,

Our rehearsal dinner was great. It left us with a lot of nice memories, and we really appreciate your having it for us.

It was so nice to spend time with the people we are closest to—before the rush of the wedding day hit!

Thanks to you, Lisa and I had a wonderful time, and I know everyone else did too. You must have spent hours making the arrangements for just the right place, the nicest decorations and the most delicious menu!

We will always appreciate your hard work, and it means so much to us that you went out of your way to make it a special night. Thank you!

With all our love,

Jim and Lisa

#10 For a bottle of expensive wine

Dear Jeff,

Thanks for the bottle of Dom Perignon! Dan and I were impressed that you thought we deserved something this expensive! We decided to save it for a special occasion—our one week wedding anniversary. Sharing it will be the perfect way to celebrate our first week of married life.

You can be sure that we'll savor your gift, and we'll toast you while we enjoy it! Thanks again for thinking of us.

Affectionately,

Deb and Dan

#11 For a special gift, such as one hand made

Dear Lin,

I know that I could never begin to make a bedspread as beautiful as the one you gave us. The colors are stunning, and the pattern is the most magnificent I've ever seen. How did you think of such a special design?

Bob is so impressed, both with the spread and with the idea that you created it just for us. We both can't express how much we appreciate such a thoughtful, lovely gift. We'll always treasure it. You're such a wonderful friend. Thanks again and again.

Love,

Jen and Bob

#12 For a special gift, such as one hand made

Dear Mr. and Mrs. Rhodes,

Pat and I just love the beautifully carved statue that you sent us. The fact that Mr. Rhodes carved it himself makes it even more special. The life-like details and delicate design will make it the showpiece in our new apartment. It will always have a place of honor in our home.

We're so sorry that you couldn't make it to the wedding because we wanted to thank you in person. Many many thanks for this beautiful gift.

Sincerely,

Jillian Swanson Hubbard

#13 To a person who gave a shower

Dear Barb,

I can't remember the last time I had such a good time. That was the nicest wedding shower I have ever attended—I'm so glad it was mine!

The decorations were perfect. Where did you get the idea of using our baby pictures? As always, you served the most delicious food. And best of all, I had as much fun playing games as I did opening the gifts!

Thank you again for the wonderful day.

Love,

Jennifer

#14 To a person who gave a shower

Dear Mary,

Thanks so much for everything. I can imagine the hours you must have spent preparing for such a lovely shower. It was perfect and I felt just like a little girl at Christmas! It means so much to me to have a special friend like you. I can't tell you how grateful I am for all you have done.

Love,

Peggy

#15 To a person who gave a shower

Dear Cheryl,

Thank you for the wonderful shower. You and Carol did a beautiful job, and I appreciate the time and effort that it took from your other interests.

Ken was especially impressed by the food and decorations and light hearted fun. I don't know what he expected, but he claims that he had such a good time he would like to attend every shower I go to from now on!

We received so many lovely gifts, all thanks to you. You're a great friend, and we will always remember this, and the many other kind things that you have done for us.

Love,

Cindy

#16   To a bridesmaid

Dear Linda,

Tim and I are so glad that you were able to be such a special part of our wedding. Thank you for all of your help, and for 'being there' whenever we needed you. It meant so much to both of us.

We appreciated the generous check. We've picked out a mirror that will hang perfectly in our hallway. it is full-length, with carved pine trim to fit my plans for the 'country look'. Come on over and see it—I know you'll love it too!

Thanks again for everything!

Love,

Becky

#17   To an usher

Dear Phil,

Thanks for doing such a great job as usher for our wedding ceremony. Several guests complimented us on the dignified way you escorted them up the aisle.

Marilyn and I especially appreciate how you left the reception to go back and get the guest book we'd forgotten! I'm glad that you're a friend I can always count on. Thanks again for everything!

Your friend,

Fred

#18 To a groomsman

Dear Kevin,

David and I know how busy we kept you
at our wedding. Thank you for being so
patient with us! Between chauffering guests,
running last minute errands, and escorting my
cousin Sherry—you must have been as tired as
we were when the day was over.

A million thanks for all that you did, you
were a huge help to us on our special day.
We couldn't have asked for a better
groomsman, or a better friend!

Fondly,

Judy and David

#19   To the Maid of Honor

Dear Kathy,

Did you know what a big job you were taking on when you agreed to be my maid of honor? I am so grateful that you did, because I don't know where I would have been without your support.

You helped me with so many of the millions of decisions I had to make. You gave me a beautiful shower that I'll never forget. You calmed my nerves before I left for the church. You solved the disaster of my torn veil before the reception. You passed on your festive mood to the guests as they went through the receiving line. You were there for me every time and any time. You were the best maid of honor that any bride could have.

I can't begin to thank you enough for all that you've done. I can only say that I am so grateful to have you as a friend!

Love,

Sarah

#20   To the Best Man

Dear Rob,

If you ever decide to be a full time 'best man' just let me know. I'll tell the world what a great job you did!

I don't think anyone will ever forget my bachelor party—you sure know how to throw them! And I'll always appreciate the way you organized the other groomsmen, making sure they knew how to put the tux on, and what to do with themselves after that.

It was so great having you worry about the little details [like looking for the rings] so that I could concentrate on my terror before the ceremony. Seriously, you were a big help in keeping me calm.

You were the best—thanks for being there.

Ted

#21   To Parents

Dear Mom and Dad,

Our wedding was a wonderful celebration and it wouldn't have been possible without your help. Greg and I know that it wasn't easy for you, but somehow you found a way to make it very special.

It was such a beautiful ceremony, and the reception was a magnificent party that we'll always remember. Our wedding day was just one big happy occasion, and we know that so much of it is because of all of your work behind the scenes.

You are such wonderful parents, who could be luckier than us? We hope someday that we'll be able to repay your loving generosity. Thank you again for everything.

Love,

Debbie and Greg

#22   To Parents

Dear Mom and Dad,

First, Patty and I want to thank you again for the microwave oven. It was a generous gift, and I know that we'll be using it often. With two careers and night classes to juggle, I don't know how we'd have time to eat without a microwave to cook in!

We are also very grateful for all of the help and moral support you gave us over the last few months. This has been a crazy, hectic time and it was great to know that we could stop by for some of your calming influence.

I hope that our marriage will always be as loving and enduring as yours has been. You two set a great example, and we hope to follow it!

Again, thanks a million for everything.

Love

Matt

#23 Special assistance

Dear Uncle John,

Jim and I will always be grateful for your generous contribution. Without it, we never would have had the wedding of our dreams. It was so thoughtful of you to offer your assistance as soon as we announced our engagement. You told us then that you wanted our wedding to be a perfect celebration. Thanks to you, it was.

We will never forget how you made it all possible. As we treasure our wedding memories in the years to come, we will always remember how you helped to make our dreams come true. Again, thank you.

With love and affection,

Tina and Jim

#24 Hosted Wedding Guests

Dear Joe and Elaine,

Thank you for the beautiful oil painting! It has such a lovely scene. We are truly overwhelmed by all that you have done for us. We will hang this painting over our couch, and will enjoy viewing it for years to come.

We are also very grateful to both of you for opening your home to my uncle Mike and cousin Walter. They are still raving about your good cooking, wonderful hospitality, and beautiful yard!

There aren't words to describe how we feel about the two of you. How did we ever get lucky enough to have you as friends? *Thank you* again and again.

Love,

Chris and Doug

#25 Took Wedding Pictures

Dear Bob,

Thank you so much for taking all of the pictures of our wedding day. It was such a wonderful gesture, and a gift we will always treasure.

You also did a beautiful job. The pictures are fantastic! John and I really think that you could be a great photographer. We don't think that anyone could have taken nicer pictures.

It means so much to us that you set aside your own chance to enjoy the party so that you could create photo memories for us. Thanks to you, we will always have a very vivid scrapbook of our wedding day.

With affection,
Laurie and John

#26 Provided Reception Music

Dear Cousin Dave,

Thank you for preparing all of the musical tapes for our wedding. You did a tremendous job, and we're still hearing praise about our music!

Kelly and I know that this project took hours and hours of your time. Knowing how busy you are, we are very impressed that you managed to get it done. It was truly a wonderful gift, and I don't think we can ever thank you enough.

Your grateful cousin,

Tom

#27 Wrote Special Prayer

Dear Uncle Ron and Aunt Mary,

Thank you so much for the elegant table linens. They look very impressive on our new dining room table. We can't wait for you to come over for dinner so that you can see them! We also wanted to give you our special thanks Uncle Ron, for offering such a beautiful prayer before dinner. It meant a great deal to both of us, and it seemed to fit the mood of our wedding perfectly. Thank you for writing it just for us. We plan to have a copy of it mounted and framed so that we may treasure it always.

Again, many thanks for all that you have done. We're looking forward to seeing you soon!

Love,

Connie and Rick

#28 To the Minister

Dear Reverend Payne,

Jeff and I would like to thank you for the lovely service you offered for our wedding ceremony. Both the prayers and the sermon were so beautiful, and included everything that we had hoped to have on our wedding day. Thank you for making this very important day a special one.

Sincerely,

Mrs. Jeffrey Allen Smith

#29   Floral Arrangements

Dear Chris,

Al and I really appreciate the beautiful job you did by creating all of the floral arrangements for our wedding.

It was a wonderful gift of your talents, and you truly outdid yourself in the most magnificent flowers we've ever seen. Everything was perfect, from the bouquets to the centerpieces. Thanks! A million thanks!

Your generosity means so much to us. We'll never forget all that you have done.

With affection,

Lisa and Al

#30   Sang at Ceremony

Dear Diane,

We are so very grateful for the wonderful gift you gave us on our wedding day. No couple could have asked for a more beautiful song medley at their wedding ceremony. Thank you, from the bottom of our hearts, for giving us that joy.

So many people have complimented us on your singing—we wish you could have heard them all. You have a wonderful talent, and we want to thank you again and again for making our wedding so special.

Love,

Terri and Don

#31   Read at Ceremony

Dear Jim,

Thanks for the classy silver salt and pepper shakers. They have a pretty fancy design—I guess they'll add some class to our next pizza party! Just kidding of course, we like them a lot.

By the way, why were you so worried? You did such a great job reading from the bible at our ceremony that a stranger would think you did it every day!

Laurie and I really appreciate your taking on that job, and you did it very nicely. Thanks for being a special part of our wedding, and for the great gift!

Your friends,

Dan and Laurie

#32   Handled Guest Book

Dear Cindy,

Thank you for taking the time to make sure that our guests signed the register. We wanted to have a record of all of our wedding guests, and thanks to you we will!

It was very sweet of you to handle that for us, and we appreciate it very much.

Your cousins,

Kathy and Ken

#33   Wedding Consultant

Dear Patty,

Thanks for making my wedding possible. I really mean that. I never knew what a wedding consultant did, but I sure do now!

I never would have made it, couldn't possibly have had anything close to the wedding I wanted without your help.

Because of your time, patience, understanding and organization—I had a perfect wedding day.

Thanks again—you're one in a million!

Best Regards,

Mary Beth Clary

#34   Not sure what gift is

Dear Cousin Paula,

Thank you for the lovely china piece. The hand painted flowers that decorate the edges are the nicest we've ever seen. John and I plan to keep it on our coffee table so we can admire it often. We appreciate the time and care you must have put into your selection.

Your cousin,

Connie

#35   Not sure what gift is

Dear Mr. and Mrs. Kentland,

Eileen and I can't thank you enough for the beautifully carved wooden statue. It looks pretty exotic on our new end tables! I know that it will receive admiring comments from everyone who visits our apartment.

We are so happy that you will be coming to the wedding, and are looking forward to seeing you there.

Best Regards,

Thomas M. Peterson

#36   New Address

Dear Bob

Jeff and I can't thank you enough for the beautiful pine clock. It will look so attractive in our new living room! I can't believe how well it matches the trim on our end tables. How did you know?

Don't forget that we'll be moving September 1st. Our new address will be:

4367 Main St.
Apartment 14-J
Midland, IN 44444

Come by and see us soon! And thanks again for giving us the perfect clock!

Your friends

Ann and Jeff

#37 Group Gift

Dear Friends,

A million thanks to all of you for the wonderful vacuum cleaner. It's such a generous gift, and Tim and I needed it desperately. This way, we'll have the house cleaned in no time. But then what will we have to complain about? Seriously though, it's just what we need, and your thoughtfulness means a lot to us. Thanks again—and see you all at the wedding!

Cordially,

Carol and Tim Davis

#38 Group Gift

Dear Co-Workers,

Thank you so much for the set of luggage! Now Dan and I can honeymoon in style. How did you ever guess that we desperately needed these?

We are truly grateful for this gift, and we can also use it if I win the contest to Hawaii this year! Seriously, your thoughtful generosity means so much to both of us. Thanks again and again.

Love,

Ann Milton

#39   Group Gift

Dear Mrs. Melton,

It was such a wonderful surprise to receive an entire set of pots and pans from you and the other neighbors! Dave and I are so very grateful for this generous and useful gift. We'll have plenty on hand for every meal, and we'll think of you often as we use them.
Thank you for giving us just what we needed!

With affection,

Kim and Dave Crane

#40   Returned Gift

Dear Anna,

We'd both like to thank you for the attractive table lamp you sent. It was an interesting choice, and we appreciate the time you must have spent selecting it.
Did you have a good time at the wedding? We didn't get to see much of you, but I hope that you enjoyed your evening.
Thanks again!

Sincerely,

Cheryl and Doug

#41 Wedding did not take place

Dear Mr. & Mrs. Michaelson,

John and I decided to call off our engagement. To be honest, we are both glad that we came to this decision before the wedding took place.

Thank you very much for the handsome canister set. It was a lovely choice and I appreciate your thoughtfulness in selecting it. I'm sure you can understand why I feel I must return it to you.

Sincerely,

Kelly Ann Richards

#42 Marriage quickly annulled

Dear Mr. & Mrs. Jackson,

Kathy and I have had our marriage annulled. It's never easy to end a marriage, but we are both better off to have quickly discovered our mistake.

I truly like the antique brass lamps (enclosed) that you had given us, and will always appreciate your thoughtfulness. I am sure you will understand why I am returning them. Thank you.

Best Regards,

Joseph M. Miller

#43 Broken gift

Dear Aunt Marilyn and Uncle Ron,

Thank you for the attractive crystal pitcher. The gold band on the edge matches our other crystal pieces perfectly! John and I appreciate your thoughtful choice, and we hope to develop the talent you have for choosing such beautiful items.

With love,

Laurie and John

#44 Unusual Gift

Dear Uncle George,

Ken and I were delighted to receive your gift. We had never heard a car horn that plays "Here Comes the Bride"! It is certainly an original and clever idea. We'll be sure to play it for you when you come for the wedding.

It will always remind us of the special uncle who chose it just for us. Thanks again!

With Affection,

Debbie and Ken

#45 Unusual Gift

Dear Rob and Diane,

Thanks so much for the lamp! Sally and I have been showing it to all of our friends. It is definitely an eye-stopper, and sure to be a conversation piece whenever we have company. We have so much fun together, we want you to be among our first guests. Please visit us soon! Thanks again.

Love,

Rich and Sally

Chapter Seven

General Letters

#46 Blanket

Dear Mr. and Mrs. Roberts,

Thank you for the beautiful green blanket. It's so attractive, and we know it will keep us nice and warm this winter! It's just the kind that Fred and I wanted, and it fits our new bed perfectly. I know we will appreciate it for years to come.

Sincerely,

Melissa Stone

#47 Picture Frames

Dear Aunt Margaret,

We are very grateful for the attractive set of enamel picture frames. The floral trim is a perfect match to the colors in our bedroom!

Soon they will be hanging in our room with our wedding pictures inside. And each time we glance at them we'll be reminded of your generous gift. Thanks again!

Love,

Kim and Rob

#48 Silver Serving Platter

Dear Ms. Townsend,

Thank you for the finely detailed silver serving platter. Ted and I were enthralled by the intricate design and exquisite detail! We plan to give it a place of honor in our apartment.

I hope that our home will always be as warm and pleasant as I remember yours to be. Again, many thanks for the delightful gift.

Truly yours,

Jillian Wright Kelly

#49 Decanter Set

Dear Sarah,

   Tom and I are dazzled by the decanter set!
It has such a gorgeous design, and the crystal
is so sparkly we just love to look at it. It looks
stunning next to the other pieces we have
received. You can be sure that it will always
grace our table when we entertain special
guests. You two are the greatest. Thanks a
million!

Love,

Pam and Tom

#50 Musical Figurines

Dear Stephanie,

   What beautiful musical figurines! Craig
and I think they are the most charming
gift we have received. The life-like detail is
amazing, and the sound is so clear and
pretty!
   Thank you for selecting such an
exquisite gift. We will truly treasure it
always.

Best Regards,

Barb and Craig

#51   Brass Candlestick Holders

Dear Stacy,

   We received the brass candlestick holders-thank you! They are so beautiful, and they were just what we needed to make our dining room table look elegant. Jeff and I both love them, and plan to add more brass pieces when we can. These will be perfect for any occasion.
   Thank you so much for the very special gift.

Fondly,

Cindy Smith and Jeff Miller

#52   Crystal Vase

Dear Mr. Jones,

   Thank you for the beautifully etched crystal vase. It is truly the most lovely I have ever seen. Jack and I hope to have it filled with brilliant flowers all of the time.
   It has inspired me to plant flowers in pots along our patio, in hopes of growing a continuing supply!
   Again, many thanks for a very enjoyable gift.

Truly yours,

Linda Maris Wilson

#53 Crock Pot

Dear Mr. and Mrs. Miller,

Because Kathy and I plan to share the housekeeping responsibilities I was really glad to see the crock pot that you sent! Now, when it's my day to cook, I can start dinner before I leave for work— and have it ready when I come home!

I know that Kathy plans to use it often too, so you can be sure that this is one gift that we will be thankful for every day.

We appreciate your taking the time to send it, and only wish that you could be in town for the wedding.

Sincerely,

Don and Kathy Reynolds

#54 Embroidered Table Cloth

Dear Mrs. Thompson,

Thank you so much for the magnificent table cloth. The embroidered pattern is so exquisite—it will be an heirloom that we know we will pass on to our children. It is such a generous gift, and we are looking forward to using it for our most special dinners.

We will think of you often as we enjoy it's beauty. Again, many thanks. It is such a considerate gift!

Sincerely,

Mrs. Barb Rhodes

#55 Picnic Basket

Dear Greg and Monica,

We really love the lined wicker basket that you sent. How thoughtful of you to fill it with picnic supplies!

Dave and I can't wait to use it, and we only wish you could be here to join us for a wonderful picnic by the lake. We'll think of you every time we use it. Thanks again for a delightful gift!

Fondly,

Jill

#56 Place Mats

Dear Mrs. Paine,

Thank you so much for the attractive place mats. They match our tablecloth perfectly! Rich and I are so pleased—they are just what we wanted.

I can't wait to meet you at the wedding so I can thank you in person!

Sincerely,

Pamela Edwards

#57 Glassware

Dear Linda and Phil,

We were so excited to receive your gift. We needed the glassware very badly, and we were impressed by your lovely choice. The sculptured pattern is perfect, and it matches the design on our dinnerware too! We will enjoy them for years to come.
Thanks again for the wonderful and useful present.

Affectionately,

Mary and Bill

#58 Set of Personalized Coffee Mugs

Dear Mrs. Johnson,

We always felt that you have a special knack for doing things that have the nicest touch! Thank you for the lovely set of personalized coffee mugs. They are good-sized, just what we'll need in the mornings. And putting our names on them will make them extra special to us.
Thanks you for giving us such a lovely and thoughtful gift.

Very truly yours,

Lorraine Williams and Carl Martin

#59 Special Recipe Book

Dear Aunt Jeannie,

Thank you so much for the book filled with all of your best recipes. It was so kind of you to take the time to record them all, and Mickie and I are looking forward to testing them in our own kitchen!

The next time you come to town, you must come for dinner. We'll cook your favorite lasagna—now that you've given us your secret! Thanks again!

Fondly,

Karen and Mickie

#60 China Place Setting

Dear Mr. and Mrs. Williams,

Bill and I were delighted to receive a complete place setting of china. Thank you so much!

The pattern and style is just what we wanted, and we will certainly feel very elegant when we use them.

We can't wait to see you at the wedding. Keep your fingers crossed for nice weather—an outdoor wedding is always such a risk!

Thank you again for giving us such a lovely and generous gift.

Best Regards,

Rita Jones and Bill Kelly

Appendix

Gift Ideas

There are many ways of saying 'thank you', and it is customary to present your wedding attendants with a small token gift in appreciation for being a part of your wedding. Many couples today also give their parents a small gift in gratitude for their assistance in the wedding. Most importantly, you and your new spouse will probably want to give each other a special gift for your wedding day. Here are some ideas for those gifts:

Female Attendants: Usually the gifts are presented at either the bridal luncheon or the rehearsal dinner. Try and personalize the gift with names and dates engraved. The maid of honor is usually presented with a distinctive gift. If you have the time, you can make each gift yourself. It will be an especially nice touch that your attendants will appreciate.

Necklace	Bracelet
Earrings	Locket
Charm	Pin
Perfume	Belt
Stationery	Purse
Wallet	Key ring
Jewelry box	Embroidered scarf
Framed photo	Pen and Pencil set
Business card holder	Watch
Hand-made items	Music box
Needlepoint box	Coffee mug
Small floral arrangements	Name plate
Engraved letter opener	Lighter

Flower Girl

Necklace	Bracelet
Earrings	Locket
Charm	Pin
Jewelry box	Music box
Purse	Watch
Framed photo	

Male Attendants: The gifts are usually presented at the bachelor party or the rehearsal dinner. The best man would receive an extra special gift. Personalize the item with your names and wedding date if you can. If you have a hobby such as wood-working (and the time), you can make each person a distinctive gift.

Money clip	Key ring
Pen and pencil set	Jewel or stud box
Pocket knife	Tie clip
Shot glass	Stationery
Playing cards	Cuff-links/Studs
Tie	Pocket flask
Coffee Mug	Beer stein
Belt	Wallet
Framed photo	Bar jigger
Business card holder	Name plate
Engraved letter opener	Change dish
Lighter	Collar bar

Ring Bearer

Tie clip	Belt buckle
Belt	Pocket knife
Accessories box	Watch
Framed photo	
Monogrammed handkerchiefs	

Parents

Have your thank you note engraved on a plaque
Framed wedding invitation
Framed photo
Small album of wedding pictures
Flowers

Spouse: Give your spouse a personal momento shortly before the wedding, perhaps after the wedding rehearsal. It doesn't have to be an expensive gift. It could be just a token with special meaning to both of you that your spouse will cherish.

Wife

Necklace	Earrings
Pin	Locket
Antique jewelry	Watch
Jewelry box	Coffee mug
Luggage	Car

Husband

Money clip	Key ring
Pen and pencil set	Tie clip
Cuff-links/Studs	Watch
Coffee Mug	Ring
Collar bar	Luggage
Car	

Other: If there is anyone else who made an extra effort for you during this time, you might want to send them a little gift, or an arrangement of flowers after the wedding. You can send it with your thank you note.

Index

About the Author

Pamela Piljac is a former wedding consultant and financial manager. She is the author of the best selling wedding books: *The Bride to Bride Book* and *Newlywed*. She has also written a guide for working women everywhere, entitled: *You Can Go Home Again*. She has been married for twelve years, and is currently working on a book about Mackinac Island, Michigan.

The Secret to Making Your Marriage Work

You have to get off to a good start. Believe me, it isn't as easy as you might think. Most divorces happen during the first year of marriage and none of those couples thought that it would happen to them either.

How can you make your marriage last a lifetime? You want to be happy, but you don't always know the best way to go about it. You may not be sure how you can avoid problems before you begin.

You can learn everything you need to know from the hard-won experience of other married couples. They have survived the blissful but stormy days of early marriage. They share their secrets in a book called NEWLYWED and teach you how to make your marriage a lasting success. This open, friendly and entertaining guide will give you a fascinating peak behind the closed doors of their married lives. Through their example, you can make your marriage as successful as theirs have been.

NEWLYWED will help you to stop the fight that all married couples have. It will show you the best way to create the marriage of your dreams.

Learn how you can make the best possible life together from the beginning. You'll find an order coupon in the back of this book. Send for your copy right away!

Other Titles From Bryce-Waterton Publications That You Will Enjoy:

It is always helpful to obtain fresh insight and guidance during important times of your life. These informative books are both practical and fun to read—an investment that will make your life easier. Order today—and dont't forget your friends!

NEWLYWED: A Survival Guide To The First Years Of Marriage

When one out of two marriages fails, how can a newly married couple avoid divorce? By learning to identify the special problems they face during the crucial years of marriage, and laying the groundwork for a strong and lasting relationship. This book will help them to recognize problems before they occur, and take steps to make their marriage a successful one. Packed with ideas and advice for making everyday decisions concerning money, home, and family, **NEWLYWED** is an important first purchase for all married couples!

YOU CAN GO HOME AGAIN: The Career Woman's Guide To Leaving The Workforce

Can a woman have a fulfilling lifestyle without struggling up the corporate ladder? This book will answer that question and more. Making this career choice is a big step, and today's woman needs to be prepared in order to adjust properly. While pondering her decision, she wonders. . . What would I do all day? Would I enjoy staying at home? Can I be 'just a housewife'? This informative book will deal with all of her concerns, and help her to make a smooth transition to a lifestyle with new and satisfying challenges. A must for every working woman.

THE GROOM TO GROOM BOOK

This unique guide for the bewildered groom-to-be will spark his interest in the wedding plans. Packed with advice from previous grooms, this practical and informative planner covers every topic from rings to receptions. Included are: A complete budget guide; planning timetable; legal/business affairs; charts; illustrations, and much more. Now, he can fully enjoy all of the wedding activities, and turn a hectic and emotional experience into a carefree celebration.

THE BRIDE TO BRIDE BOOK

Since its appearance on the wedding market, this book has become one of the most popular wedding planners available today! A complete wedding consulting service at an affordable price, this book is packed with practical ideas, money-saving tips, examples, illustrations, and worksheets that will help the bride-to-be avoid problems, save money, and make the right decisions for a perfect wedding day.

BRIDES THANK YOU GUIDE

Saying "Thank You" will be easy and fun with the help of our handy guide. It provides many helpful ideas, and over 75 examples and suggestions to make your job easier. You'll want to acknowledge each gift received, and show gratitude to those who helped make your wedding day a special one. It's not what you say, but how you say it, that means so much to the giver.

Order Form

Bryce-Waterton Publications
P.O. Box 5512, Dept. T 90
Portage, Indiana 46368

Please rush me the following books:
Newlywed .... $8.95 _____
You Can Go Home Again .... $9.95 _____
Groom-to-Groom Book .... $7.95 _____
Bride-to-Bride Book .... $9.95 _____
Bride's Thank You Guide .... $5.95 _____
    Sales Tax (Ind. residents only) .... _____
    Shipping .... _____
  *Shipping: Add $1.50 per book
**Check or money order in U.S. funds only.

I understand that I may return any book for a full refund if not satisfied.

Name: _____

Address: _____ Apt. _____

City & State _____ Zip _____

Charge to my (please check appropriate box)
☐ Visa   ☐ Mastercard
Account number (list all numbers on card):

— — — — — — — — — — — — — — —

Interbank number (Mastercard only) __ __ __ __

Expiration date: _____

Signature